IF YOU
ASK ME

IF YOU
ASK ME

(And of Course You Won't)

Betty White

BERKLEY
New York

BERKLEY
An imprint of Penguin Random House LLC
penguinrandomhouse.com

Copyright © 2011 by Betty White

ISBN: 9780425245286

The Library of Congress has cataloged the G. P. Putnam's Sons hardcover
edition as follows:

White, Betty, date.
If you ask me: (and of course you won't)/Betty White.
p.   cm.
ISBN 978-0-399-15753-0
1. White, Betty, date.   2. Television actors and actresses—United States—Biography.   I. Title.
PN2287.W4577A3 2011   2011007358
791.4502'8082—dc22
[B]

G. P. Putnam's Sons hardcover edition / May 2011
Berkley trade paperback edition / February 2012

Printed in the United States of America
17th Printing

Photo research by Laura Wyss, Wyssphoto, Inc.
Interior photo credits: Page ii—Charley Gallay/London Entertainment/Newscom.
Front cover photo of the author copyright © by Kwaku Alston for stocklandmartel.com.
Back cover photographs (clockwise from top left): copyright © by Bettmann/Corbis;
copyright © by CBS Photo Archive/Getty Images; copyright © by Donald Sanders/Globe Photos,
Inc.; copyright © by NBCU Photo Bank.

Gratefully Dedicated

to

Loretta

Marysue

and

Bruce

Contents

LOVE AND FRIENDSHIP

ANIMAL KINGDOM

STATE OF AFFAIRS

SINCE YOU ASKED . . .

Foreword

One time I remember hearing someone ask my friend George Burns, if he had read a certain book, current at the time.

George said, "I can't read a book cuz I'm writing one."

We all laughed — George could make anything sound funny — but he was absolutely right. Whatever else you may be involved in, writing a book takes precedence. There is that inexorable due date staring you in the face.

By my sixth book you'd think I would know better, yet once again I was thrilled when they asked me to do another one.

I simply love the process. And not just because I can do it sitting on the couch with my shoes off and my dog by my side.

Writing is my favorite thing.

Betty White
2/14/11

BODY AND

MIND

GROWING OLDER

O ld age isn't for sissies."

"I can't believe I'm getting old."

"Why do people ever say 'Happy Birthday'?"

And the list goes on—we've heard them all. However, if one is lucky enough to be blessed with good health, growing older shouldn't be something to complain about. It's not a surprise, we knew it was coming—make the most of it. So you may not be as fast on your feet, and the image in your mirror may be a little disappointing, but if you are still functioning and not in pain, gratitude should be the name of the game.

Actually—and don't laugh—there may even be some upsides to aging. People treat you more gently. They may even think your years of experience make you wiser than you are. And <u>somebody</u> always finds you a place to sit down, whether you want it or not.

Somewhere along the line there is a breaking point, where you go from not discussing how old you are to bragging about it. I have never lied about my age, but these days I seem to work it into the conversation at the drop of a hat. Please stop me before I get to the point of, "Hi, I'm Betty White—I'm eighty-nine years old!" There's nothing to brag about—I didn't accomplish that age, it sneaked up on me.

There is even a funny side to aging, if one has a warped sense of humor.

If one has no sense of humor, one is in trouble.

I joined the American Women's Voluntary Services
when World War II broke out.

ON
REFLECTION

*I*n show business, the mirror obviously plays a big part in one's life, but early on—long before I started working—my beloved mother taught me another role the mirror plays. I can still hear her:

"Bets, you can lie to anyone in the world and even get away with it, perhaps, but when you are alone and look into your own eyes in the mirror, you can't sidestep the truth. Always be sure you can meet those eyes directly. Otherwise, it's big trouble, my girl."

It may sound like a cliché, I realize, but oh, it's so

true. On rare occasions I have tried to prove my mom wrong. I stare back at my reflection and try to rationalize my way out of something, but it never works. Those eyes in the looking glass take on a life of their own.

It still works, Mom. Even after all these years.

My beloved mom—Tess White.

Animal lover that I am, I am often handed animals by pet owners at events and appearances, like this cute little devil.

HEALTH

As the years add up, I am so grateful for the good health I have been blessed with, and I don't ever take it for granted for a second. I make it a point to never let my weight vary more than five pounds in either direction; I wear glasses to read or to drive; I have a two-story house and a bad memory, so all those trips up and down the stairs take care of my exercise.

I had my eyes done in 1976 and have let nature take its course ever since. As for my hair, I have no idea what color it really is, and I never intend to find out. My mother's hair never went gray, it just went mousy. So when mine started going that way, I just started tinting it and haven't stopped. And I never will!

In terms of my weight, I weigh myself every morning. And if I go up one pound, I take it off the next day. It's easy to take a pound off, you just skip something. But if it goes to three pounds, it becomes more difficult and one of them usually just stays there. Or five pounds—even worse—sometimes those just stay. I watched it happen with my mother. So I figure it's easy to just take them off immediately, and it's not too much of a sacrifice.

I don't have a sweet tooth, but I do have a cocktail before dinner. I also love french fries and hot dogs. The famous Pink's hot dog company in California actually named a hot dog after me, and since I eat mine plain with no condiments, it's the Betty White "Naked" Dog. So if my weight goes up a pound or so, it's easy to find something to cut out to bring it back down.

My obsessive addiction to crossword puzzles I chalk off as mental gymnastics. I love games and puzzles. On the set of *The Lost Valentine*, a Hallmark movie, Jennifer Love Hewitt and her boyfriend, Alex Beh, and I played Scrabble during every lunch break. And I always have a book of crosswords or acrostics in my purse wherever I go. Whenever I've had a puppy, I've put newspaper down for him, but if I put down a piece of the paper and there's a crossword in there, I'll snatch it right up and say, "No, you can't go on that!"

I subscribe to the Crosswords Club and the Puzzle Club and get a new set of puzzles every month. They were given to me as a gift, and I renew them all the time. I have stacks piling up. I won't <u>live</u> long enough to do all these puzzles, but it's a comfort zone for me.

And no, you can't use a dictionary or an encyclopedia—that's a cheat.

I'm not a big pill-taker, and almost never have a headache. But I once read an article about Dr. Linus Pauling, who took vitamin C every day to stave off colds. I thought, If it's good enough for Linus Pauling, it's good enough for me—why not? I asked my doctor, and my doctor said that's rubbish, vitamin C has nothing to do with the common cold. But I wasn't taking any other vitamins, so I started taking vitamin C every morning. I haven't had a cold in twenty years.

I attribute my generous supply of energy to DNA—my father was so filled with energy, my mom used to call him "Horace the Hummingbird." She'd say, "Honey, could you light long enough to sit down?"

I'm grateful to have inherited that gene. But in the end, the energy is also very much due to enjoying what

I am so lucky to do for a living. Show business. If all this sounds too "Little Mary Sunshine," please put up with me while I celebrate it.

Human nature being what it is, I'm ashamed to say that even with all the good stuff, there are still days when the misgivings move in. Maybe when I'm overtired or overloaded—or over_something_. In spite of myself, I find it harder to roll with the punches. I get irritated inside and begin to feel that I'll never catch up. When this happens, I try desperately to resist indulging those ungrateful moods, and I try to attack any one of the many things that need doing, but it just doesn't work and I don't accomplish a damned thing. It might take a little while to shake those doldrums.

It's been widely reported that I prefer the company of animals to humans. As a matter of fact, Barbara Walters asked me that direct question in an interview at one point. With Barbara, you don't hedge.

I said, "Yes, that's true!" Now, here with you I want to be on the level: It _is_ true.

Can you blame me? Animals don't lie. Animals don't criticize. If animals have moody days, they handle them better than humans do.

Next time I'm feeling overwhelmed, I think I'm going to start channeling my dog Ponti.

I moved to Chappaqua, New York,
for a spell after marrying Allen Ludden.

SENSES

Sooner or later, some of our senses lose a little of their efficiency. (What do I mean "some"?! What do I mean "a little"?!) Eyesight, for example.

It sneaks up on you.

Reading and needlepoint have been passions for me since I was a child, and as middle age approached, I tried not to notice the fact that my eyes were gradually changing—things weren't quite as sharp. I'm not sure how long I could have gotten away with ignoring it if it weren't for my husband, Allen Ludden.

Since we first met, my romantic fella had always had a delicious habit of leaving little love notes for me in unexpected places (I still have them all), so I wasn't surprised one night when I turned the bed down to find a greeting card under my pillow. It said, "If you can't see I love you . . ." I opened the card to find ". . . SQUINT!" I laughed hard, but the next day I headed for the eye doctor.

Okay, so you get your glasses and everyone is extremely supportive. "Oh, those are very pretty." "Those glasses look great on you!" Et cetera, et cetera.

Somehow it's a different story when your hearing starts to go. People can even seem a little annoyed when you say "What?" too many times. They'll repeat themselves, but frequently without making it one jot clearer or louder. You find you need to see faces. If someone turns away while still talking, you realize how much lip-reading you'd been doing without realizing it.

I can remember accusing my dad of selective hearing—hearing only what he wanted to hear. Shame on me. That was before I learned how isolated one can feel when she misses a key remark and loses track of the conversation but is loath to admit it.

My father never enjoyed parties and avoided them whenever possible. He always said he couldn't hear anybody in a crowd. I always thought it was because he just didn't like parties. But now I understand. Cocktail-party small talk may not be much worth hearing, but it's tough when you can't hear it at all.

Sorry, Daddy, for this late apology—now I understand.

Daddy—Horace White.

A scene from Bringing Down the House *with Steve Martin.*

HUMOR

At the Screen Actors Guild Awards, my agent, Jeff Witjas, and I got there a little early, because I was presenting an award with Alec Baldwin (and, lucky me, this meant I didn't have to walk the red carpet!). So we arrived and went straight to the greenroom to wait.

We're sitting on the couch when Tim Conway walks in.

Now, I am such a pigeon for Tim Conway. I look at him and I can get hysterical.

So Tim walks in, and he looks at Jeff and says, "Don't get up," and he looks at me without changing his inflection at all and says, "And I know you can't."

Jeff and I broke up laughing (not Tim, he plays it straight).

Some people think they have a tremendous sense of humor. They make a remark and look at you and say, "Did you get it? Did you hear what I said?" And it just kills the humor altogether.

For me, humor is about rhythm. It's like an ear for music. It's hard to explain.

For instance, at the table reads each morning for *Hot in Cleveland*, you listen to learn the timing. You hear the other characters, and you know where they're coming from, and it helps you map out the show—it puts you way ahead of the game for rehearsal. It's listening for that beat, like with music.

You go through the table read, and you just feel, *Wait one beat*. Or, *No, less time, don't wait that long beat—say it quickly*. If you think about it too much, you screw up the timing completely.

I think what helped my comedic timing most were those breakfasts and dinners growing up—I was raised with such funny parents who told marvelous stories. I'd be sitting there as a kid, wanting to add to the conversation, wanting to jump right in with an idea, but if I blurted something out it might ruin the moment. It taught me a lot about the power of waiting.

Still, sometimes something hits my brain and my mental editor falls asleep and it comes right out and it's simply less funny than it would have been had I waited a beat.

I remember being on set with Allen and trying to explain it to him once, listening to him deliver lines and thinking, *Oh, he should wait a beat.*

But he kept doing the scene the same way, kind of rushing through it. I was cringing.

When I finally mustered the courage to mention it to him, he did not take it well. That's an example of when a wife and husband shouldn't work together! I kept my mouth shut after that.

Another good example of the importance of your mental editor!

ENTHUSIASM

I think everybody needs a passion.

Whether it's one passion or a hundred, that's what keeps life interesting.

If you live without passion, you can go through life without leaving any footprints. You might leave behind pleasant memories in the minds of friends and acquaintances, but those dissipate quickly.

You often hear about people who can't wait to retire. When they're sixty-five years old—that's when they'll start to live. And I think it's so sad! My father was a workaholic who just could not stop <u>working</u>. He would talk about all the things he was going to do when he retired at sixty-five, and you knew he was whistling in the dark. And sure enough, he died at sixty-four and a half. He just couldn't face it.

I'm so fortunate that I not only have a passion for my profession but that that profession allows me to indulge my other passion—for animals—and work for their welfare. If I was in any other profession, people might not listen to me.

I know I'm fortunate, and boy, am I grateful.

I rarely hear the alarm clock. Even when I have to get up early, I'm usually awake before it goes off. I need about four hours' deep sleep and I'm good to go. I chalk it up to my passions and enthusiasm. I can't imagine living any other way.

With Bandit, aka "Bandy"—I later named my
production company after him!

HOLLYWOOD

STORIES

At the 2011 Screen Actors Guild Awards with the girls
from Hot in Cleveland*—Valerie Bertinelli, me,*
Jane Leeves, and Wendie Malick.

HOT IN CLEVELAND

Sixty-three years in this business and I still find it difficult to refuse a job offer. That could be a hangover from the early days when jobs were hard to come by and I always thought each one might be my last.

I do manage to utter the "NO" word if the schedule is on overload or if the script doesn't appeal to me—the latter being the real issue.

Not long ago, I agreed to do a guest stint on a new pilot, and I insisted on the proviso that I would not be involved if it got picked as a series. It was to be a one-shot only, because my schedule was packed.

The pilot was called *Hot in Cleveland*, starring Valerie Bertinelli, Wendie Malick, and Jane Leeves. Now, it can often take months to learn the fate of a pilot, but after only three weeks the show got an order for ten more episodes from TV Land network. It was the first original scripted show TV Land had ever done—they were best known for rebroadcasting many of the old classics.

When the producers asked me if I would do a couple of additional episodes, I reminded them of our agreement and reluctantly explained that my calendar was just too full, but thank you <u>so</u> much.

Of course, I wound up doing all ten shows!

Actually, the pilot had been a delightful experience. The girls were a joy, the writing was fun, and it had been a very happy set. What's to walk away from?

The TV Land folk were very pleased at the warm public response to the show. So pleased that as we finished the tenth show, I got a call from my agent, Jeff Witjas.

"Betty," he said. "Great news! They've picked up *Hot in Cleveland* for twenty more shows!"

I remember holding the phone for a moment. Then

I said, "No, Jeff, that wasn't the agreement. My schedule hasn't let up. I don't know how I could possibly do it!" Here I should mention that the taping schedule for a television series is four or five days a week, requiring me to be on set sometimes for ten hours a day! "Much as I love the show and the company, I'm still on overload," I told Jeff. "There's no room whatsoever to work in a series!"

P.S. Guess who signed on for all twenty episodes?

I have the backbone of a jellyfish.

I'd say I was a pushover if I wasn't so delighted.

And that was before the show received two SAG nominations and was rated the number-one television show on cable. *[Editor's Note: Sorry to be a ratings-dropper.]*

What absolutely boggles my mind is that I find myself in yet another hit series, having a ball with a <u>wonderful</u> cast and crew. One of those in a lifetime is a blessing, two of them is a privilege, but three out of three?

I owe Someone, big time.

With Larry Jones, president of TV Land.

Hosting Saturday Night Live.

SATURDAY NIGHT LIVE

*B*etween doing a Snickers commercial to be run during the Super Bowl, hosting *Saturday Night Live*, and starting a new series, *Hot in Cleveland*, 2010 turned out to be, as they say, a very good year. As a result, people keep congratulating me on my big "comeback" or "resurgence." Thanks, guys, but I haven't really been away—I've been working steadily for the past sixty-three years. Granted, since those gigs, some folks may feel they've gotten something of a Betty White overdose.

It was a huge and wonderful surprise when the Snickers commercial turned up as the first spot on the Super Bowl. We didn't expect that when we filmed it one early, cold California morning. The idea was, I was playing football with a group of nice young men. (Tough duty!) It wound up with me being tackled into a pool of icy, muddy water. A great stuntwoman took the actual tackle, and I just lay down in the puddle in the same position where she had landed. She took the dive, but I got the laugh. Sure doesn't seem fair, does it?

At nearly the same time that the Snickers ad was making waves, I was hit with another surprise. Years ago, I had turned down the hosting job on *Saturday Night Live*—three times! I feared that this Californian would be like a fish out of water on such a New York–oriented show. I said "No, thank you," and never gave it another thought.

All these years later, seemingly out of left field, in January 2010 there was a campaign on Facebook called "Betty White to Host *SNL* (Please)," started by a young man named David Matthews. By March, apparently almost half a million people had voted! And that's when Jeff Witjas came to me with the hosting offer from *SNL* producer Lorne Michaels.

My reservations hadn't changed a whit, but Jeff, who

With the great ladies of Saturday Night Live.

is not only a dear friend but has judgment far better than my own, would not take no for an answer. He insisted I <u>had</u> to do it. Over my strong (and desperate) objections, off we went to New York.

It was a terrifying proposition from the word "go," but Lorne Michaels brought in the wonderful Tina Fey, Rachel Dratch, Ana Gasteyer, Maya Rudolph, Molly Shannon, and Amy Poehler (at the time, as pregnant as you can get) for the show, and they could not have been more supportive or more fun to work with. Ditto Lorne Michaels.

At the start of the rehearsal week, there are maybe forty or more sketches in the mix. These gradually narrow down to the five or six that make the cut by show-time on Saturday.

Normally, I memorize my lines. But with forty-plus sketches to weed out, that was impossible, and I was told we'd be using cue cards (anathema to me). That only added to the panic.

In fact, I think that scared me more about *SNL* than anything else, because I don't use cue cards and I don't use teleprompters. (Maybe for a commercial, which is a whole two pages long. Then the teleprompter is wonderful, because you look right into the lens.) But cue cards I hate, because it usually means your eye switches

More scenes from Saturday Night Live.
Note the costume changes!

NBCU Photo Bank

as you look from the camera lens to the card, lens to the card.

So when it came to *Saturday Night Live*, I thought, *How am I going to do that?*

Well, they have this wonderful card man who knew my reservations. He stood a little above and behind her with the cards, and said, "Keep your eyes on me and the cards. Don't look at Tina Fey."

I'm thinking, *How can you play a scene with Tina Fey and not look at Tina Fey?*

"Don't look at Tina and your eyes won't move and you'll be fine. And she's doing the same thing," he said. "Trust me." I did, and it made all the difference.

If you watch the show, you'll see that even some of the most accomplished actors around have that eye switch that is so distracting. And these are stellar actors!

But the cue cards were just one part of the elaborate production that is *SNL*.

The week before, you fly into New York and go to the studio, and you sit around the table with all the cast and read forty-one sketches. You've not seen a script—this is your first look at the material. Everybody reads their parts, and as you go through them, some are naturally weeded out because they're just not working. Then

More scenes from Saturday Night Live.
Note the costume changes!

NBCU Photo Bank

Lorne Michaels does his edit and weeds more out. Maybe twenty make the blocking stage.

I was so nervous, but Lorne brought Tina Fey and Amy Poehler and all those wonderful gals to read with me, and they couldn't have been more supportive. Soon, of course, we began having fun. (At the time, Amy was so pregnant she could hardly fit in the sketch. She has since had a beautiful baby boy. Now when I see her I say, "Have you lost weight?")

As the week progresses, so does the weeding. By the day of the show, it has been whittled down to five or six sketches!

That day, you run through the show two times—in full costume. But it's more than a dress rehearsal, it's the real show, twice.

The challenge for me, besides the cue cards, involved the complete costume changes for each sketch, which must be done in one minute, thirty seconds. *Saturday Night Live*, indeed!

They have been doing this long enough to have it all down to a system, so the only thing one can do to help is to do absolutely nothing. As a sketch ends, someone grabs your hand and drags you offstage into a very small closet nearby. You are literally attacked as someone strips off your clothes and stuffs you into new ones while someone else is touching up your makeup and yet someone else is removing your wig and pinning on a new one. (Ouch!) Your hand is grabbed again to drag you back onstage, too frazzled to remember <u>what</u> the next sketch is until you get back to those blessed cue cards.

Jeff, who was standing just offstage, says all I did was glare at him as I flew by. "I didn't know you could look that fierce," he told me.

The day after the show aired, on the flight back to Los Angeles, I had to admit it had been an exciting and incomparable experience.

"Thank you, Jeff. It wouldn't have happened if it weren't for you," I said.

Jeff replied, "Well, it's about time!!!"

And as chance would have it, *Saturday Night Live* brought me my seventh Emmy Award. The day it was announced, Jeff called, wanting to know, Didn't I think <u>he</u> deserved the Emmy?

Truth be told, he absolutely should have accepted the award.

With my castmates from The Mary Tyler Moore Show—
Ed Asner, Mary Tyler Moore, and Ted Knight.
The show won twenty-nine Emmys.
© BETTMANN/CORBIS

AWARDS

I know it sounds like a cliché, and I've discussed it in
my interviews and other books, but it's the truth—
I truly believe a nomination in and of itself is the greatest honor one can receive for one's work.

When you're nominated, you get it all sorted out
in your mind—not <u>who's</u> going to win, but that you
yourself are <u>not</u>. And that's not being coy—that's being
realistic.

At the Screen Actors Guild Awards in 2011, I was
nominated for Outstanding Performance by a Female

Actor in a Comedy Series, and the actors with whom I was nominated were simply extraordinary—Tina Fey of *30 Rock*, Jane Lynch of *Glee*, Edie Falco of *Nurse Jackie*, Sofía Vergara of *Modern Family*, and me for *Hot in Cleveland*. When I saw the competition, it took all the nervousness away. I thought, *This is great, but I'm never going to win!*

So when my name was announced, I was simply stunned. I'd nearly forgotten I was nominated. And if you think I was in shock, you should have seen Jeff Witjas. He looked at me, and the color just drained from his face. Meanwhile, the girls from *Hot in Cleveland* were jumping up and down with excitement—they were, if possible, more delighted than I was!

As with the instances when I've won previous awards, it all happened so fast. There's always a striking and sudden contrast: one minute, you're sitting at the table, wherever that may be, and the next you're onstage. You've been sitting in the audience long enough that you know your environment around your table, you know who's seated nearby, but you get up those steps and turn around, and suddenly you see the whole overview of the audience. And that's overwhelming, because you haven't thought of all those people in that great big auditorium. You've thought only about the tables nearby.

When you turn around, the impact of what you see scares anything out of your head that was ever there!

I've never, in all the instances I've been nominated for an award, prepared a speech. I've known whom I would thank, but I've never actually written a speech. And this occasion was no different. And as in times past, I opened my mouth and words came, and God knows what they were. But it is such an exciting feeling.

When I picked up the SAG statue itself, which presenter Jon Hamm had left on the podium for me, it felt like it weighed twenty-five pounds. All I could think about was that it was the heaviest award I'd ever held.

Allen's always there when I win an award, or when anything special happens, because nobody would celebrate it like he did. So he was right up there with me.

Ever wonder what happens to an actor after they accept an award and leave the stage?

After you win, someone escorts you backstage to a room filled with press. They all ask you questions and take photos. Then, if it's early enough in the program—which it was, at the SAGs—they'll take you back to the table. That was great, because the girls were so excited. I think Valerie was still jumping up and down, bless her.

We had also been nominated for the show itself, for Outstanding Performance by an Ensemble in a Comedy Series. That was the one I wish we had won rather than the individual, but my castmates didn't seem to care one bit.

My beloved castmates couldn't have celebrated more.

Actors tend to take the bows for their performances and forget to share the credit with those who put the words on the page. Where would we be without them? To be blessed with good writing is such a privilege, and I have been so lucky. Shows like *The Mary Tyler Moore Show* and *The Golden Girls* have lasted over time thanks to some of the best writing in the business, and I am ever grateful.

The morning after the SAG Awards, we had a table read for *Hot in Cleveland*. Suzanne Martin, the creator of the show, who does a lot of the writing, walked in and said, "Welcome to the <u>award</u>-winning *Hot in Cleveland*!"

It was a great moment.

Completely stunned at the
2011 Screen Actors Guild Awards!
KEVIN WINTER/GETTY IMAGES

NAME-DROPPING

At the 2010 SAG Awards, I was honored with the Life Achievement Award.

I got up from the table, and once again I had that moment of sudden contrast—when I got up to the podium, I turned around, and here's this enormous Shrine Auditorium audience. It's just overwhelming.

When I gained my composure, I tried to explain that being in show business is like living in a small town.

Your paths really cross and cross again through the years.

Even if you've not seen someone in a long time, all of a sudden you're working with him or her again.

I talked about how two show-business people who encounter each other might not <u>know</u> each other, but they're automatically in the same club, and they greet each other like friends.

And I talked about how I've <u>never</u> gotten used to running across a celebrity. I'm always impressed. I've never outgrown it. I still remember the thrill I had the day I came home and there was a message that Fred Astaire had called. <u>Fred Astaire!</u>

So I said to the audience . . .

"I look out here and everybody is famous. And I've had the privilege of knowing many of you and working with some of you—I've even <u>had</u> a few of you! You know who you are."

Afterward, as I was led back to my table, George Clooney was at the podium. He saw me walking across the room and said, "And while I'm here, I'd like to thank Betty White for her discretion."

At the 2010 Screen Actors Guild Awards.
My friend Sandra Bullock presented me with
the Life Achievement Award.
KEVIN WINTER/GETTY IMAGES

TURNING
DOWN ROLES

I'm often asked if there are roles I was offered that I regret turning down.

The answer is <u>No</u>.

Sure, I've turned down parts in movies that went on to be successful.

One was *As Good as It Gets*.

But in that movie, there was a scene in which a character throws a dog down a laundry chute. When I read the part, I told the director, James Brooks, who is amazingly talented, "I just can't do that!" I know it's for laughs, but given my feelings about animals and my work for animal welfare, I just didn't find it funny. I didn't think it would be a good example to people who might try it in real life.

I was hoping that Jim would change it! But Jim had fallen in love with the scene and wouldn't change it. So I said, "Sorry, I can't do it. But thank you very much!"

Another script was sent to me, and it started with a truly disgusting scene in which a drunken Santa Claus is vomiting all over a stack of toys. I didn't find that funny, either. The scriptwriters were these really talented guys, but I said, "Thank you but no thanks!"

So the answer is, more than regretting <u>not</u> taking a role, I feel good that I've turned down roles for the right reasons.

With Leslie Nielsen in Chance of a Lifetime.

OLD FRIENDS, NEW STORIES

*I*t's always a joy to know your castmates.

I've known Carl Reiner for years. Lately, he's been appearing on *Hot in Cleveland* as a guest star in a recurring role—my character's boyfriend, no less.

Carl Reiner and Allen were in the Army together in World War II in the Pacific. I met Carl one night years later, when Allen had all the guys from his outfit over to our house. There was Mort Lindsey and Howie Morris and Harry David and Carl. No wives were invited. So I fixed a couple of big casseroles for the fellas and took the dogs upstairs to the bedroom. I wasn't allowed downstairs—it was one of those guys' nights out.

Carl recently told me, "I wouldn't have a career without Captain Ludden."

I had no idea what he was talking about, and said so.

Carl told me about this entertainment group Allen was in, called the Army Entertainment Section. Carl had written some material and stood up one night in front of the guys and read it.

Allen said, "You've got to do more of that."

Maurice Evans was also in the outfit, so Allen got Maurice to take the material to a producer, and Carl was off and running. He continued to be a writer but also went on to become one of our great comedians. It took a Shakespearean actor and a game-show host to make it happen in the beginning, but Carl took it from there.

Today, every so often, Carl will say to me, "Wouldn't Allen get a kick out of this if he were here—seeing us working together?"

I don't tell Carl, but I think Allen is getting a kick out of it, because he's never very far from me. Ever.

With Carl Reiner on the set of Hot in Cleveland.

THE
RED CARPET

Several times throughout this opus, I mention how much I love this business I'm in. And I mean every word of it.

But for all the things I enjoy about it, if ever I'm asked if there's something I <u>don't</u> like, the answer is a resounding <u>Yes</u>.

Red-carpet events.

Don't get me wrong. When I'm at home watching television, I love seeing who's there and what they're wearing. But when you're the walkee, it can be an absolute nightmare.

In real life, you step out of the car and immediately you're struck blind and deaf as you're greeted by a line of photographers armed with flash cameras and microphone-wielding television reporters, three deep, all shouting at you.

Betty!

Betty!

Over here!

Betty, look here!

Look up, Betty!

Mrs. Ludden! (They know that will get my attention!)

With all the flashing lights and the noise, you tend to lose your balance. All of a sudden, you're staggering and you're sure people are thinking, *Oh, she's had a few!*

The lights are glaring and the noise is horrendous, but you try to be as polite as possible, because these aren't villains, they're just people trying to do their jobs.

Sometimes the function has somebody who takes you down the carpet. For instance, TV Land will send someone if the four of us are doing the event. But always, I also have Jeff walking behind me, at the edge of the media zone, off the red carpet. Riding shotgun, which I need.

Historically, premieres have always had these red-carpet events. But the process has taken on new proportions of late. Every event has a system of protocol, and the number of stars and reporters and photographers and media outlets just seems to grow and grow.

It feels like everyone's there with a microphone. And I know a lot of them—we do interviews all through the year. So as you're stumbling around, you're trying to talk to all sorts of different people. Usually a representative from the project (whatever project it may be) guides you to various reporters along the way—likely, they mix and match us along the way, to be fair to all the outlets. But you can't really hear what they're saying, given all the noise, so you just keep talking and hope you're making some kind of sense. It's all seat-of-the-pants.

You can't resent it—it's a necessary evil to promote a project. It's a hazard one just has to get over.

It's not my favorite part of my job. Have you noticed?

I would rather go to the dentist for a root canal.

*The TV Land folks threw me an eighty-ninth
birthday party. Here I am with the girls
from* Hot in Cleveland. . . . *The red
carpet is a lot better with friends!*

D DIPASUPIL/FILMMAGIC.COM

With Malin Akerman, Ryan Reynolds, Sandra Bullock,
Anne Fletcher, and Mary Steenburgen
on the set of The Proposal.

THE PROPOSAL

Doing movies is different but interesting.

One thing in particular struck me about being on the set of *The Proposal*—what a joy it was to work with Sandra Bullock.

Here's this big movie star, and there wasn't anything "movie star" about her at all. She was just as down-to-earth as she could be. We became great and dear friends. Still are. The same goes for Ryan Reynolds.

Anne Fletcher, the movie's wonderful director, had been a choreographer originally. We all got relaxed and silly with one another, so she wouldn't just walk onto the set—she'd do a ballet leap onto the set, saying, "The director is here!"

In one of the scenes in the movie, Sandra and I are dancing around a bonfire.

On that day of filming, we'd been working all day, but we had to finish that night, because we were moving locations the next day. It was three o'clock in the morning, and I had to sing this blinking Eskimo song in order to shoot the scene.

First I had to learn it. And Eskimo makes no sense. I don't know how Eskimos communicate! But I learned it. God knows what I was really saying.

And then it came time to dance around the fire.

Anne just turned us loose—told us to do whatever we felt like doing. And Sandra's such a good sport. So just about the time we started moving around . . .

Drip.

Drip.

Drip.

The rain started, and it kept getting harder and harder.

Now, we had to finish this scene! We were leaving the site the next day. So they put up a canvas on four big poles to keep us dry. But the rain continued—harder and harder.

I've said before I love my profession, and I do. At three o'clock in the morning in the rain, you'd better love it a <u>lot</u>.

With Sandra—a scene in The Proposal.

THE LOST VALENTINE

For the Hallmark movie *The Lost Valentine* with Jennifer Love Hewitt, we shot in this pretty little house in Atlanta in a lovely neighborhood. Across the street was a low wall, and behind it was this big grassy lawn.

All the neighbors knew that I was working there, so they all brought their dogs.

We'd look across the street from the set, and they'd all be lined up—owners and dogs, sitting on the wall.

Between scenes, I'd go across the street to say hello and get to know all the dogs.

There was this young man, Mitch, hired to escort me around the set, who would go over with me. One day he came in and said, "Betty, there's a Newfoundland out there."

The way he tells it, at the word "Newfoundland," I <u>shot</u> out of my chair like a bullet! Why not? I don't get to smooch with a Newfie that often.

So I got my dog fix every day.

Now, that's a happy set.

With Jennifer Love Hewitt on the set of the
Hallmark movie The Lost Valentine.

LETTERS

INTERVIEWS
(REDFORD)

*I*t is a real privilege to have been working in this
business for so long, but there are a few built-in
hazards—some of which can't be avoided. Interviews,
for example. There is no way to even estimate the number of them I have done over the years—we must be in
the millions by now. This means I have answered the
same questions, told the same anecdotes, wheezed on
and on ad infinitum, again and again. The interviewers
know the material better than I do, going in—and it's
tough to put a fresh spin on it.

A few years ago I was asked one of the standard
questions for probably the umpteenth time: "Is there

anything you haven't done in your career that you would still like to do?"

Well, I had just seen Meryl Streep and Robert Redford in *Out of Africa* for the third time, so the answer was automatic: "Yes, Robert Redford." And I was surprised to suddenly find it was true! Ever since, I have realized that that answer fits a variety of situations, and I have used it accordingly.

I have never met him. I never want to meet him (I'd be too embarrassed after taking his name in vain so many times). However, what began as a crush on a movie star soon grew into genuine admiration. I became aware of his concern for the environment, his love of and respect for nature, his involvement with The Wilderness Society, and I maintain that the Robert Redford answer works for me in almost any department.

Fast-forward to January 2010. A few days after I had received an unbelievable honor from the Screen Actors Guild, I brought the mail in one morning, as usual, and found the following letter.

Dear Mrs. Ludden:

Robert Redford has asked that I forward his congratulatory note to you on receiving the

*Lifetime Achievement Award from the Screen
Actors Guild.*
    Cheers to you!

                        Sincerely,
                        Donna Kail
                        Assistant to Robert Redford

More than a note, the congratulation consisted of a delightful, <u>funny</u> six-stanza poem that began with "Dear Betty" and ended with "Congratulations, Robert."

By now I don't have to tell you how my mind was blown. Of course, my first reaction was that someone was putting me on, but the stationery was authentic, and on looking further, I found a great picture of himself, signed "Guess who? Robert Redford."

Finally, I found the courage to write him a thank-you and said I couldn't promise to stop using his name—unless he didn't find it funny.

I can only say that Robert Redford is one class act.

P.S. I know you would love to hear the poem. Sorry.

With Bandit, Dancer, and Stormy.

WRITER'S
BLOCK

Certain common clichés maintain that most men love hardware stores, just as women dote on shoe stores. I have no idea how accurate that is, because, personally, I am strange for stationery stores. Not for the fancy writing paper—it's those tablets and packs of lined three-hole notebook pages and those packs of typing paper that turn me on. I even buy those things when I go to the grocery store, whether I need them or not.

Let's say I am in the middle of a writing project and have, perhaps, hit a slow spot. Bringing in this stuff can recharge the battery. Or, if I am <u>not</u> in the middle of a writing project, it can often cause me to start one.

Why? I have no idea, but it has been that way all my life—even back to my school days. A fresh pack of paper was the best incentive in the world for me to tackle my homework.

As weird as all this sounds, I am not alone. I can remember once being told by an author—who was rather well known at the time—that on the rare occasions when he hit a stubborn writer's block, there was only one specific brand of green-lined paper that could get him started again. He called it his "paper laxative." As soon as he'd bring in a pack, the ideas would start again.

Okay, so I'm weird. At least I am in good company.

John Steinbeck, who was Allen's and my good friend, did his writing standing up at a drafting table—in longhand, his white bull terrier, Angel, lying across his feet. People always seem amazed that I write in longhand. Well, if it's good enough for Steinbeck, it's good enough for me! I really can't communicate to a machine—the thoughts want to go from my brain

down my arm to my hand to the page. After I've written
that first draft, I copy it over again onto another page.
That's when the most changes are made, as I polish and
rewrite the original—once again, in longhand.

My mother had beautiful handwriting
her entire life. As a little kid, I
loved the times with her when I would
make her write something so I could
see how closely I could copy it. It
wasn't a learning chore, which I
probably would have resisted. It
was a game.

Somewhere in those fun sessions
she managed to make a point that
has stuck: handwriting is a means
of communication. Why not make
it as easy to read as possible?

I still remember those lovely times with my mother when I would try to copy her handwriting. Maybe it isn't only John Steinbeck's influence after all.

With our computers today, we have a whole new population who will find all of this totally academic, since they write by hand as little as possible. Even signing their names seems to have gone by the boards.

Computers can't take all the blame. Both my business manager and my doctor have handwriting that is practically unreadable. Whenever I get fan mail in which the handwriting is absolutely illegible, I wonder if they've taken writing lessons from my business manager!

Ironically, when I grew up and entered into show business, I found many people who actually practiced diligently to make their autographs as eye-catching, illegible, and uncopyable as possible!

On *Hot in Cleveland*, Valerie Bertinelli, Wendie Malick, Jane Leeves, and I sign scripts each week to be used as charity auction items. I am always so grateful that I know their names, because I wouldn't have a clue from their signatures, which are as distinctive and interesting as they are. You can't imagine how dull my readable but boring "Betty White" looks on that script cover in that distinguished company.

I must practice.

Betty White Betty White Betty White Betty White

Tess, my mom, of the beautiful handwriting.

FANS AND
FAN MAIL

T he term "fan" somehow seems more appropriate for one in the faceless crowd at a sporting event than for those nice folks who greet me on the street, or in the market, or at the airport—or wherever. The greetings are warm and friendly, probably because they have been inviting me into their homes for decades.

The Betty White Fan Club, Bets' Pets, has been around since 1971. While it has grown some over the years, it is still kept very personal, thanks to long-serving president Kay Daly and charter member LeElla Moorer.

They have hung in there since the very beginning and have become treasured personal friends.

Over all those years, Kay and Lee have attended almost every performance I've done, not only in Los Angeles but out of town as well. As of today, they are in the audience every week when we shoot *Hot in Cleveland*. They are deeply appreciated.

Bets' Pets was so named because from its inception, the club was dedicated to helping animals. The members pay minimal annual dues, and at Christmas and for my birthday in January, they put together a bonus gift—all of which is forwarded to various animal charities in my honor. They are a great group.

As well as sending out newsletters to the members about my activities, Kay manages to put out a great journal every year, comprising pictures and articles and pet news sent in by club members, which keeps us all updated on one another. She did all that while working as a fourth-grade schoolteacher until she retired. Lee, after serving as a nurse in the military, became head surgical nurse at UCLA Hospital until her retirement. I am most grateful that they haven't retired from my life!

Fans, in general, continue to amaze me. When I'm working out of town and I show up at different studios for appearances, no matter which city we are in, there is always a group waiting, holding pictures of me to be autographed. <u>How</u> do they know my schedule when I hardly know it myself? Time is always short, and I feel bad when sometimes they rush me past and I can't stop and sign, but these people always seem to understand and keep smiling.

Fan <u>mail</u> is something else again, with which my invaluable assistant Donna Ellerbusch and I contend! We try to keep up, but the mail continues to burgeon. A good percentage of it consists of picture requests, which I sign for Donna to send. I can't answer it all, of course, but there are a few categories that Donna sets aside, to which I do respond: those who have just lost a life partner and need to share their pain with someone who has been through it; boys and girls achieving Eagle Scout and the Gold Award, respectively; hurting individuals reporting the loss of a beloved pet; and students writing me as part of a school project. My answers are understandably brief, but answer I must.

Fellow actors have urged me to send the mail to companies that make a business of handling fan mail rather than complicate a busy schedule. One actor friend maintains that he never deals with his fan mail in <u>any</u> way—he just dumps it.

Truth be told, I need to read these letters to discover

what I'm doing right or, more important, <u>wrong</u>, and these writers don't hesitate to tell you.

[Editor's Note: My life has changed dramatically since I began writing this book.]

I used to be able to travel alone without thinking about it. I can't do that anymore. I have to have a meet-and-greet on both ends to get me through the airport. People are just being nice, but recently I actually missed a plane because I couldn't break away.

Between the Snickers commercial and the explosion of projects on which I worked in the past year, and a whole generation of fans who have met me through syndication, it seems like the number of people who call themselves fans just keeps growing. (There was a time when *The Golden Girls* was on four times a day!)

I don't mean for this to sound self-serving, but it can be a problem, and yet these are the people responsible for your good fortune!

Please know how grateful I am. Even if I do have to rush by to catch a plane!

With Dancer.

GLOBE PHOTOS

STAGECRAFT

RANGER

One of the first questions in every interview since I started in television more than sixty years ago has always been, "When you were growing up, did you always want to be in show business?"

My answer has never changed. As a kid, show business wasn't even in the mix. As far back as I can remember, I wanted to be either a forest ranger or a zookeeper. The problem was, back then a girl wasn't allowed to be either one.

That was a real problem for a girl who grew up the

way I did. Even <u>today</u>, my earliest, fondest memories are of the pack trips in the High Sierras on horseback I took every summer with my mom and dad. Mules carried our camping equipment and food supplies. The first time we went, I was just four years old and rode in front of Daddy on his horse. The following year I graduated to a mount of my own.

It was a two-day trip to our destination, Rae Lakes. (Today, you may be able to drive there—I don't want to know.) Once there, we pitched camp, put bells on the horses and mules, and turned them loose. Pros that they were, they all hung out together nearby.

I can still hear those bells.

The next day, the guide would leave us and corral the animals to take them back to the ranch. Three weeks later, he'd bring them back in to pick us up. In those days, we would never see another human during the whole three weeks—it was true wilderness. Heaven.

After those earliest years, we moved our campsite to a remote area of Yellowstone National Park. In the way a lot of kids look forward to Christmas all year, I used to count the days from one June to the next, until we could take off again.

On the last half-day of school for the summer, my folks would pick me up at Beverly Hills High School, and we were on our way. Dad always wore a forest ranger hat on vacation, and when I'd spot that hat, I would know the day had finally arrived.

So it's no surprise that I developed a love of animals and the outdoors, but as a child I could only dream of becoming a zookeeper or a forest ranger. Today, after forty-seven years of working with the Los Angeles Zoo, I am satisfying the zookeeper part. Now, let me tell you the clincher.

Not long ago I received a letter from the United States Forest Service that thrilled me to my toes. It seems someone there must have read one of those interviews about those early dreams, because there was an invitation to Washington, D.C., where, in a special program at the Kennedy Center, the Forest Service would make me an Honorary Forest Ranger! It was all very official, and I couldn't believe my eyes.

Of course, I went back for the ceremony, and it was a beautiful program. Thomas Tidwell, the Forest Service chief, made the presentation with a huge Smokey Bear standing behind him. As I stepped to the podium to accept, I got a big hug from Smokey, which almost got me, but I didn't actually lose it until—after receiving the certificate and the badge—they presented me with an official ranger's hat.

He's been gone all these years, but as the memories washed over me, I would swear my dad was standing right there. It is a moment I continue to replay in my mind.

My eternal thanks to the Forest Service for this honor, which is so deeply appreciated. It truly was one of the greatest moments of my life.

I shall continue to work my hardest to spread the word that not only must we protect our wilderness areas—we must appreciate them. They are an endangered species.

ASSOCIATED PRESS/CLIFF OWEN

ON STAGE
FRIGHT

I can remember my first attack of stage fright. I was in grammar school, in the third grade. And I had to get up in front of the class and recite a poem.

"Little Machi met a cameraman on a Chinatown Street one day. . . ."

That's how it started, and I was panic-stricken. I don't remember if I made it through the poem at all, but I can remember what it felt like.

Still, I somehow managed to continue as a young girl, participating in plays throughout grammar school and high school. In fact, I wrote the play commemorating graduation from Horace Mann Grammar School—which was called *Land of the Rising Sun*. We were studying Japan at the time, and like any good red-blooded American girl, I wrote myself into the lead! I also wrote a prologue for the show, explaining that it was traditional Japanese theater and props were held by non-actors. The play opened with the princess talking to a nightingale. Since one of the football players was going to be onstage holding a birdcage, clearly this all had to be explained in the prologue.

Guess who spoke the prologue?

So I was the star <u>and</u> the interlocutor. And anything else I could be. Remember who wrote it!

But I never outgrew the stage fright.

To this day, it still happens—every single time I go onstage.

Jay Leno and I are good friends, and I appear on his show all the time. We greet each other before the show and have a catch-up in the makeup room. Suddenly it's showtime. I'm in the wings and those butterflies appear. Ballplayers have rituals. They may touch each corner of

Color Day at Beverly Hills High.
I sang "Heart and Soul."

the plate with the bat to calm themselves down. I have no ritual. I have—butterflies.

So you work your way through it.

Let me be clear: <u>You are never calm</u>. But your job is to deliver.

In the case of Jay Leno, or Craig Ferguson or David Letterman or Jimmy Fallon, suddenly the conversation gets interesting and it carries you along.

Just hope the audience comes with you.

At the 2011 SAG Awards, when my name was announced, I was so shocked—it was so unexpected that I would win the award, given the other nominees, that my first thought was, *They read the wrong name.* Then I got up to the podium and thought, *Oh, no, I'm going to have to say something!* On air, I might look calm, but if you knew what was going on in my head, your own head would spin.

None of the tricks I try work. I'm lucky if I can breathe.

It's amazingly common for actors to have some form of stage fright. It just manifests itself in different ways.

I remember Rue McClanahan used to say, "That's one thing I never get! I never get stage fright!"

I think she was lying through her teeth.

NBCU Photo Bank

You're taking a chance every time you step in front of an audience.

So is the stage fright due to fear of forgetting lines? Fear of drawing a blank on what to say? Fear of making a fool of oneself?

All of the above.

Rue may have been the only actor I've known
to say she didn't feel stage fright.

TYPECASTING

After more than thirty hours a week on live television for four years, there were those who thought of me as sickeningly sweet. They'd say, "She'll make your teeth fall out!" But if we met at a party, they would tell me, "Oh, you're not as bad as I thought you were!"

I was certainly typecast as icky sweet on *Life with Elizabeth* and even *Hollywood on Television*. But then Sue Ann Nivens came along and changed the whole picture.

The neighborhood nymphomaniac on *The Mary Tyler Moore Show* was a surprise to everyone (including me)!

The character was written as "an icky-sweet Betty White type."

The casting director, Ethel Winant, said, "Why not get Betty White?" But the executives said they couldn't have me read for the role because Mary and I were best friends, and it might make it awkward for Mary if it didn't work out.

As an actor, you don't get every role you try out for, so it wouldn't have bothered our friendship at all, but they didn't know that.

Well, I guess they couldn't find anybody sickeningly sweet enough, so they finally called me one Saturday morning and explained the part of the Happy Home-maker and asked, "Would you do it?"

Of course I said I'd be thrilled!

So I called Mary and said, "Guess who's doing your show next week?"

She said, "Who?"

I said, "Me."

She said, "Oh, no, you're not! I have veto power!"

She was kidding, of course.

As Sue Ann Nivens on The Mary Tyler Moore Show.

And Sue Ann Nivens really did change my career. That sickly sweet image I'd grown up with expanded to another context. She was the Happy Homemaker who could fix anything, cook anything, clean anything, and sleep with anyone who would stand still. Another character, Phyllis (played by Cloris Leachman), became suspicious that her husband was having an affair with Sue Ann, because he'd come home with his clothes cleaner than they'd been when he left.

People would invariably ask Allen, "How close to Sue Ann is Betty?"

He'd say, "They're really the same character—except Betty can't cook."

Recently I had a similar role switch. I did a Hallmark Hall of Fame movie called *The Lost Valentine*, which is a very poignant and emotional film.

I have been doing comedy for so long that people were surprised to see me play a dramatic part. I kept getting calls afterward, saying, "Hey, I've never seen you do anything like this!"

But it's good to mix things up as an actor. Or else you can grow too accustomed to a character. On *The Mary Tyler Moore Show*, I played alongside Gavin MacLeod (as Murray Slaughter). When she was near, Sue Ann always petted Murray's bald head.

In a poignant, emotional role—with Jennifer Love Hewitt in The Lost Valentine.

Gavin went on after *The Mary Tyler Moore Show* to his own hit series, *The Love Boat*. I did a guest role on his show, and in one scene I'm standing behind Gavin, as Captain Stubing, and it was so hard not to stroke that bald head!

So for me, Sue Ann was a huge career mood change. *The Mary Tyler Moore Show* aired for seven years altogether. I came on in the fourth season, in what was to have been a one-shot appearance. The most episodes I ever did during one season was twelve of twenty-two—the other seasons, I did only five or six episodes. But people still remember Sue Ann. She was such a mess!

And such fun to play.

Allen's quip about me and Sue Ann
always made people laugh.

Sometimes you lose control.

CAST
CHEMISTRY

On *Hot in Cleveland*, when we'd all been cast and come together for our first table read, we all simply fell in love.

It was that instant rapport. We all knew one another from other shows. Everyone in the cast is a pro. Valerie Bertinelli from her career work, Wendie Malick from *Just Shoot Me*, Jane Leeves from *Frasier*, and I from *The Golden Girls*. We'd all seen one another work, so we were looking forward to getting to know one another better. But you can't manufacture chemistry—it's either there or it isn't. And boy, was it there!

When we're on the set, we're holding one another's hands, or someone will come by and ruffle the back of your hair. And we laugh inordinately.

Back in my second book, *Betty White in Person*, at one point I was writing about *The Golden Girls* and the team relationship we had. Well, I reread it recently and laughed out loud. It described the exact same rapport I was just talking about on *Hot in Cleveland*.

Let me quote:

From the very beginning we were each thrilled by the <u>professionalism</u> of the other three. No one had to be carried. Whatever one of us served up was returned in kind . . . or better.

Of equal importance, if a set is to be a happy one, we were also blessed by the work manners of our group. No one had to be waited for . . . each was where she was supposed to be when she was supposed to be there. This set the tone and allowed us to relax and get silly, knowing that when the whistle blew, we'd all be in the chute.

It's as though I wrote that about Valerie and Wendie and Jane! How can you get that lucky again, twenty-five years later?

We all just love to laugh. One night we went off the air in hysterics—we couldn't tell anyone what the joke was. We still can't. Valerie came in, early in the season, with this not-nice joke and we all found it so funny that before each show we put our arms around one another and say, "One for all and all for one"—and then we add the punch line. And it works every time.

I feel so fortunate to be on another show with the rare chemistry and goodwill that I experienced on *The Golden Girls*. It feels a little bit like lightning striking twice.

But I'll take it.

With the Golden Girls—Bea Arthur, me,
Rue McClanahan, and Estelle Getty.

On The Late Late Show *with Craig Ferguson.*

STAND UP?

*P*eople often mistake me for a comedienne and ask me to do stand-up routines for charity. But that's not my skill set. I'm an actor, not a comedienne. Doing stand-up is an entirely different beast.

Witnessing good stand-up makes you appreciate what people like Craig Ferguson and David Letterman and Jay Leno do every single night, night after night. Sure, they have writers, but they have to put their stamp on it, too. Night after night. Did I mention that?

I asked Craig once, "Are you getting a little road-weary?"

And he said, "Not all the time."

When you're a guest on one of these shows, you're successful when there's great repartee. Now, we know the hosts are accomplished comedians, so the question is, can guest and host play well together?

The producer has some assistant call you for a pre-interview, which I hate. The assistant calls, and then you end up giving your whole interview to them, and you don't want to repeat it when you're on the air! It's obviously a safety net for the host, so he has something to fall back on.

But when I'm on Craig's show, we never go near those notes. He's got them all there on his desk, but we just start talking.

Usually when I appear on his show, I'm doing a sketch involving some kind of costume, and I'm always short of cash. That's a running theme. But recently I was on and we didn't have any idea where we were going.

And Craig, like Tim Conway, is one of those people you have trouble making eye contact with for fear of cracking up. He has these eyes that just dance. So when I'm on his show, on the couch, I talk to him looking down at the floor, and he talks to me peering intently into my eyes.

So we sat down and just started having this easy conversation, and we didn't know where we were going or how we were going to end, but somewhere along the line it just got funny. I can't tell you how or when, but it did. And then it just came to its natural end. So at the end, the crowd was clapping and laughing, and he hugged me and whispered in my ear, "We did it! What did we do?"

It goes back to that repartee and comedic timing both. You have to listen and play off what someone else says. You can't be thinking of what you're going to say next or it dies right there. If you listen to people, it triggers something in you to which you can respond. It's about both really listening and hearing that funny track that you can pick up and deliver back.

I can't tell you it's innate. I don't think it is. But I think you have a propensity for it. And after that, practice helps a lot.

But this is not stand-up comedy.

With comedy, as opposed to drama, you get an instant review. With a dramatic performance you act up a storm and hope it works.

Doing comedy—if you don't get the laugh, you know you bombed.

It's a tough business.

NBCU Photo Bank

THE CRAFT

When a script comes to me, I read through the whole thing so I know what the story is about, who the other people are, and where they're coming from. It gives me an overview.

Then I go back and start learning.

I have trouble acting with a script in my hand, so I memorize as quickly as I can to get both hands free.

Other actors that I've worked with are more comfortable holding their script through dress rehearsal, like a security blanket. Everyone works differently.

On a series, every week it's inevitable that at some point someone forgets what the next line is. In front of a live audience, there is that deadly silence. You all look at one another, wondering, *Is it me?* So we just stop and start to giggle in spite of ourselves, which spreads like wildfire in the audience. We have a good (??) laugh, then we just go back a couple of lines and start where we were before.

Similarly, if you stumble or your tongue gets twisted, you can stop and start up again with the line before, and the editors can make their magic.

Though technology has advanced so dramatically and the equipment is better (since, say, *The Mary Tyler Moore Show*), the actors do it more or less the same according to whatever works for us, personally.

You go with it—and pray a lot.

Sometimes it's not all laughs—even on a comedy set. On *The Golden Girls* just a couple of weeks into the show the first season, both my mom and Bea Arthur's mother became seriously ill. Ironically, the script we were doing at the time happened to be heavily mother-daughter-oriented—just by coincidence. Two weeks later, both our mothers were gone. Not an easy time.

Line readings are always a challenge. When the line falls right, you feel it in your gut. That's how you intend to do it from then on. But just try to repeat it—you can't get it back to save your soul from perdition. Now and then, that "good line reading" doesn't happen until you're driving home after the show. But, of course, the party's over by then.

I've heard some of the best actors say the same.

It's a strange craft!

With James Lipton on Inside the Actors Studio.

BRAVO/PHOTOFEST

TELEVISION

Over time, I've turned down three Broadway shows. I love summer stock. But with summer stock, there's a beginning and an end to the production. Maybe a week's rehearsal and three or four weeks playing the show, then you're free.

If you get into a Broadway show and it doesn't work, you're a failure. And if it does work, you may be stuck for who knows how long. It just doesn't sound great to me!

My theatrical friends think I'm a Neanderthal.

"It's <u>THEATER</u>," they protest.

"I know," I say, "but I'm <u>television</u>!"

I was there when television first started. We grew up together.

When I graduated from high school, television had just begun in New York, but it hadn't yet started in California.

I had done our senior play and was asked to do an experimental television show downtown. Our senior class president and I did a scene from *The Merry Widow* up on the fifth floor of the Packard Automobile building. And it was broadcast all the way to the bottom floor. My parents had to stand in front of a tiny little monitor on the first floor to see me! But it was the beginning of television in Los Angeles.

Then I actually got paid (a little) to do a role as the girl behind the hotel desk on a show called *Tom, Dick, and Harry*. Never do a show with three comics who have a broom. But it was fun.

Al Jarvis had seen me on that, and he called and asked if I would be his Girl Friday on a TV show he was going to do. Al had had a marathon radio show, and now he was going to be on for five hours, five days a week. They soon upped it to five and a half hours a day and added Saturday. That was *Hollywood on Television*. I'd been getting paid $5 by the local station.

When Al called, I thought, *Maybe I'll get another $5!*

Instead, Al offered me $50 a week! I was shocked. Even more so when they gave me $200 per week when they extended the airtime.

For two and a half years we worked together on that program. And then, Al went over to ABC, and I inherited *H.O.T.*

You talk about experience—it was like going to television college.

One of the things I realized from the first time I ever did television was the intimacy of the audience. There are never more than two or three people watching a television program—if there are more than three people in a room, they're usually talking among themselves, not listening to you! So as a television actress, I knew my audience was always very narrow. Later, when I did movie roles, however, it was for this great big audience. And I didn't know that audience's content at all. You don't have that feeling of reaching an individual. And you <u>don't</u> look at the camera!

No matter how television has grown, you're still really just talking to those two or three people.

People greet me on the street as a friend, not a celebrity. "Hi, Betty!"

I was walking down the street the last time I was in New York, and a guy drove by and rolled down his window and hollered, "I love *Hot in Cleveland*, Betty!" Had I been a film star, he wouldn't have done that.

There's a remoteness to film stars. As an accessible television performer, you have to be careful walking down the street—you might pick up a hundred new best friends. It's so unlike film stars, it's a different genetic makeup.

Television and I discovered each other together. It was a very short window to get in, timing-wise.

I was blessed with that timing, because we were inventing as we went along in those first days of television. And I joined the parade.

On Boston Legal *with James Spader.*

LOVE AND

FRIENDSHIP

Our wedding day—June 14, 1963.

FULL CIRCLE

*L*ife does have a way of coming full circle.

As of this writing, I have just finished shooting a movie (*You Again*) starring three great gals—Jamie Lee Curtis, Kristen Bell, and Sigourney Weaver. I thoroughly enjoyed working with all three but got a special kick out of getting to know Sigourney. It was her father, Pat Weaver, who was at the time the president of NBC, where I got my first network job (*The Betty White Show*) more than half a century ago.

After several years of doing local television, going

"national" was a major turning point in my career, and it was a dream come true.

At the time, I was working five and a half hours a day, six days a week, with Al Jarvis in a live broadcast. No script—all ad-libbed—on KLAC's Channel Thirteen in the local Los Angeles area. The show was called *Hollywood on Television*.

After two years, Al left and I inherited the show and worked solo for two and a half years. Every Thursday night I was also doing a one-hour variety show that was something like a small-scale *American Idol* (like they say, there's nothing entirely "new" in this world!). It was all local. People would come on the Thursday-night show and sing, and whoever won the variety show, whoever got voted the best performer, would have a week appearing on our daytime show. Here I should mention that I would sing, too—and I don't know how they could tell me from the amateurs!

So after the five-and-a-half-hour daily broadcast on KLAC, we would hold auditions to screen the candidates for the variety show. They'd sing for us, and some you wouldn't believe—you just didn't know where to look. You'd think, *This is the longest song that was ever sung!* And you felt so sorry for these people. . . . But sometimes we'd get lucky. The most memorable winner was a young Gogi Grant, who went on to achieve a great career.

On *Hollywood on Television*, we finally got music—a guitar player named Roc Hillman. I would sing three songs each day to his accompaniment.

Then came Pat Weaver's job offer, which was a godsend. Pat warned me what it would entail:

"Do you think you can handle doing a half-hour show every day, five days a week?"

Well, after five and a half hours a day, six days a week, I wondered what I would do with all the time off! I would also have a five-piece band, led by well-known music man Frank De Vol. Roc Hillman, of course, was still on guitar.

Pat Weaver was a real mover and shaker in the television business, and many of his innovations are still extant today. It was Pat, I believe, who first divided television time into segments like on the *Today* show and *The Tonight Show*.

Little did I dream that all these years later I would be working with his star of a daughter. Sigourney wasn't even a gleam in her father's eye at that time.

Nice as he was, I was in total awe of Pat when I

worked for him back then. I must admit, at first I felt a bit of the same when I started working with Sigourney, since I have been a devout fan of hers, especially her fine performance as Dian Fossey in *Gorillas in the Mist*.

I am delighted to say that we have grown into warm and loving friends. You can't imagine how thrilled I was when I came offstage after *Saturday Night Live* to find her waiting to say hello in my dressing room. She and Victor Garber (also in *You Again*) had come over to surprise and support me. These are moments I absolutely cherish.

But it doesn't stop there.

The day before the SAG Awards in 2011, I was at an event and a gentleman approached me and introduced himself. He said, "I'm Roc Hillman's son! My dad's still alive!"

I said, "You've got to be kidding me!"

He said, "No, he's one hundred and four, and he's still going!"

Like I said, life sure does have a way of coming full circle.

On the set of You Again *with Sigourney Weaver,*
Odette Yustman, Kristen Bell, and Jamie Lee Curtis.

DATING DU JOUR

At this moment in time, it seems somewhat current and choice for women to pair up with younger men. These gals are called "cougars."

Well, animal lover that I am, a cougar I am not. All my life, even as a kid, I have preferred men older than I am.

Unfortunately, today I don't think there _is_ anyone older than I am!

Even at this age, once in a while I meet a man who seems a trifle more interesting than usual. Nothing untoward—just someone who might be fun to know a little better. I've even thought (<u>to myself</u>) that it might be nice if he asked me to lunch or dinner, perhaps. Then reality kicks in and it cracks me up. This guy is probably a much younger man—maybe only eighty—and not about to even look my way.

So I don't worry very much about whether I'm going to be asked to lunch. I know I had a rare thing in my relationship with Allen. In fact, my castmates on *Hot in Cleveland* seemed so curious about him—and asked so many questions about him!—that I finally had to wonder out loud, "Why do you always ask me about Allen?"

The answer was simple: "We love the look you get on your face when you talk about him."

ABC Photo Archives/ABC via Getty Images

LOSS

*A*llen is always with me.

The other night, a dear friend, Mark Alexander, called me to say he had seen the Hallmark Hall of Fame movie I did, *The Lost Valentine*.

He said he was surprised to see me doing something dramatic.

"At one point, when you were crying so hard, you glanced up and it stopped me cold. I knew who was in your mind."

I think the toughest thing about loss, and the hardest

challenge, is the isolation you feel in its aftermath. You spent so much time sharing your life with someone, talking through issues, even disagreeing about things, and all of a sudden there's a hole. There's nobody there and you think, *Well, who's in charge?*

My God, it's me. I have to make the decisions. I can't share the decisions any longer.

And that's tough because you don't fully trust your own judgment.

That's why it's great to have people like Jeff Witjas in my life. And why it was so great to have Jerry Martin, whom I lost just a few weeks ago. Jerry and I would talk to each other around dinnertime almost every night. I could get things off my chest that I couldn't necessarily air to anyone else.

The older you get, the fewer of those there are.

I always thought I would be the one who would go— particularly with the Golden Girls, because I was the oldest. But then we lost all of them, and I'm the only one left and I'm still functioning. I think, *How did that happen?*

MARIO ROMO/GLOBE PHOTOS

On Mama's Family *with Vicki Lawrence*
and Rue McClanahan.

FRIENDSHIPS

There are all kinds of different friendships.

With a new friend, you start to tell an anecdote and there's a whole explanation that needs to go with it so they'll understand.

But with old friends, you don't have to do the backstory, because you talk so often that they know what's going on in your life—or maybe they were there at the time.

Then there are the business friends—whose job it is to tell you where you're wrong, whereas your other friends may just agree with you.

Friendship takes time and energy if it's going to work. You can luck into something great, but it doesn't last if you don't give it proper appreciation. Friendship can be so comfortable, but nurture it—don't take it for granted.

My closest friends have always been boys or men. As a kid, I wasn't interested particularly in what the girls were talking about. I had to watch myself. I didn't want to get a reputation that I don't like women, because that's not true at all. I just like guys best.

That's not politically correct these days. But it's still fun.

With Mary.

AGENT JEFF

Jeff Witjas and I met at the William Morris Agency when I was a client. He wasn't my agent, but I knew him from the company. When William Morris began to disintegrate, Jeff moved over to APA and set up shop there.

My long-term agent, whom I adore, and who is still one of my dearest friends, Tony Fantozzi, was one of the partners at William Morris, but then he retired. So I inherited a new representative with whom I wasn't really connecting.

I kept getting calls from APA: Would I come in and take a meeting?

They weren't from Jeff, but I knew where they were generated from.

Tony, who was no longer with William Morris, said in his inimitable tough-guy Italian accent, "Why don't you take the meeting?"

So I went down to APA, and I went into this boardroom for a meeting with all their executives seated around the table. I didn't have to explain my work or what I'd done or my background. They'd all done their homework. I was really impressed by that, and very gratified. So we talked quite a bit, and then they made the formal request: Would I consider coming to the agency?

I said, "Let me think it over."

After the meeting, Tony picked me up and we went back to the Beverly Hills Hotel and had a beer and talked about it. I explained to him that I was really impressed at how they had worked at being informed about my career to date.

Tony said, "Why don't you go with them?"

And so Jeff became my representative at APA, and I haven't stopped working since.

We're a great team. He never lets me go on a trip—for instance, to New York—without accompanying me. Not just as a protector but as an arranger—he takes care of all the appearances and sets everything up while we're in town. He's a delightful travel companion, because he never lets me get overloaded but he still gives me the freedom to do things that are important to me.

On one occasion, we were spending three nights in New York. We're both fans of Chinese food, so that first night we found this wonderful Chinese restaurant and were as happy as could be. As you know, there are <u>many</u> good restaurants in New York City. So on the second night we were trying to decide where to go to eat and somehow decided to go back to the same place.

The third night, we didn't even discuss it—we just went right back to the Chinese place. And the next time we were to go to New York, he called in advance from California and set up a reservation.

It's obvious how well we get along.

When we get home, I call his wife and daughter and thank them for loaning him to me.

We have a lot in common, and I rely on him implicitly.

I trust his judgment more than I trust my own!

With my agent, Jeff Witjas, and Ann Moore, then the CEO of Time, Inc.

©PatrickMcMullan.com

ANIMAL

KINGDOM

BUTTERSCOTCH

*L*et me share another animal-related episode that I revisit in my mind from time to time, like a mental DVD.

BraveHearts Therapeutic Riding & Educational Center is a fine therapeutic riding school in Chicago dedicated to giving disabled children a new perspective, and I was invited to host their annual fund-raiser. I was familiar with BraveHearts because the former chairman of Morris Animal Foundation, Dan Marsh, and his wife, Dayle, are on the board. A few years earlier, they had enlisted my help on behalf of a beautiful young horse named Butterscotch who had terribly crippled hooves—a result of flounder, followed by a bad case of pneumonia. There wasn't money for the necessary medical procedures at the time, but Dan and Dayle made such a case for him, I couldn't resist getting involved. I underwrote the surgery and he made a complete recovery. When the invitation came to host the benefit, my first thought was *I'll get to meet Butterscotch!!* and off I went.

I arrived in Chicago the day of the fund-raiser and that afternoon was taken to the ranch for a tour of the school.

Riding therapy enables children who have spent time looking up from a hospital bed to get an entirely different view of the world, looking down from the back of a horse. They are led around a corral by a young person walking alongside. Instead of boring exercises in a bleak hospital environment, they receive the same benefits in an exciting and stimulating setting.

As the tour ended, I headed straight for the stables to find my friend, Butterscotch. They had warned me that he had a tendency to nip, but when I walked up to his stall he put that velvet nose in my hands and seemed to appreciate the kisses.

I met his trainer, Tom Chambers, who invited me to see a program he had put together, "with your pony, Butterscotch."

I followed Tom out to a large corral in the back. I was told, "Just stand still in the middle of the corral and follow my instructions." He then signaled for the other trainers to bring in Butterscotch. The red horse, however, had his own ideas and it took four burly men to finally manage to push him into the corral. He galloped at full tilt around and around inside the corral fence—with me turning to watch him, Tom standing beside me.

"Now," Tom said, "put out your hand."

I did so, palm down.

"No, palm up, for friendship."

When I turned my hand over, the horse immediately checked his pace to a walk.

"Point to him."

As I pointed, the pony stopped completely, his sides heaving.

Tom continued. "All right, now go over and pat his neck."

It was a little intimidating, but I had to trust Tom.

As I patted the heavily breathing horse, Tom said, "Turn and walk out of the corral, and take Butterscotch home."

I walked away and couldn't believe it as Butterscotch followed me, his head almost on my shoulder—all the way back to his stall!

Believe me, I'm not trying to sound like some sort of horse whisperer. I rode my first horse when I was too young to straddle, during those camping trips to the High Sierras with my parents. My horse, Queenie, was big and broad and gentle—and she wanted to eat absolutely everything along the trail. I wasn't big or strong enough to control her. The guide had to come and tell her, "Queenie, that's enough!" And shoo her along. So horse-whispering was not my forte.

With Butterscotch, Tom was doing all the work, but it was Butterscotch who was making the choices. I learned later that during the whole exercise, Tom was trying to figure out how he was going to transfer Butterscotch's attention from himself, since he'd done all the training, over to me.

This lovely horse must have said, "I can handle it—leave it to me."

Recently, I received a beautiful crystal paperweight engraved with Butterscotch's image. My heart broke when I read the note, which told me that Butterscotch had galloped on.

Godspeed, dear boy.

PHOTOGRAPH BY ALLEN BOURGEOIS

KOKO

*F*riends are always considered a blessing, but, on occasion, there may be those who are just a little extra-special in their own way.

Not because they happen to weigh more than three hundred pounds and have incredible strength, nor even because they can communicate without words, but simply because they are, well, special. As is my friend Koko.

You probably already know of Koko. You may have seen pictures of her tenderly cuddling her beloved kitten. Koko, of course, is the amazing gorilla who has learned to communicate fluently through sign language, thanks to her mentor and best friend, Dr. Francine "Penny" Patterson.

It was thirty-eight years ago that a young student named Penny Patterson was allowed custody of a baby gorilla from the San Francisco Zoo. Deeply interested in interspecies communication, Penny began an experiment to try to teach Koko to sign. Penny had struck what would become her life's work.

Dr. Patterson and Koko have lived and worked together since then in an effort to see how far Koko can come in learning and using a modified form of American Sign Language. The results have been spectacular. I have seen this firsthand, and it has been my privilege to know Koko—up close and personal.

Koko and Penny are headquartered on a lovely compound near Redwood City in Northern California. They have developed The Gorilla Foundation, committed to protecting critically endangered gorillas everywhere, whose numbers in the world continue to plummet and who, without urgently needed intervention, could face total extinction in the not-too-distant future.

The very first time I ever laid eyes on Koko, on my initial visit, was through a window of her multi-room house (it even has a restroom, which she uses appropri-ately!). As I passed the window, there was this enor-mous black face looking out at me, curious to see who was walking across her porch.

I followed Penny into a small entry area, one en-tire wall of which was chain-link, separating us from Koko's living room. Pulling a small stool over against the chain-link, Penny invited me to sit down. As I sat, my arm against the wire, this magnificent gorilla ap-peared on her side of the fence and, totally unbidden, sat down beside me, our shoulders touching.

I was absolutely ecstatic, but that was only the beginning.

We sat there for a few minutes, quietly, before Koko got up and moved along the wire wall to a floor-to-ceiling gate, outside of which Penny was seated beside a small cabinet. Sticking her finger through the wire, Koko pointed to the top of the cabinet.

Penny smiled and nodded. "Koko wants to show you her new television set. She loves to watch movies, don't you, girl? Her favorite is *Pretty Woman*." And with that, she flipped on the TV.

Letting out an irritated grunt, Koko waved her hand back and forth in a gesture that even I could interpret only as an emphatic "NO!" so Penny turned the set back off. Koko immediately started pointing at the cabinet again. Penny turned the TV back on, only to receive the same agitated negative reaction, so she turned it off once more.

Mumbling, Koko began pointing to a top lock on the tall gate, then to a middle lock, and finally to the lock at the bottom, then pointed back at the cabinet across the office once again. You could almost feel her roll her eyes in frustration.

"Oh, Koko, forgive me," Penny said, as she picked up a bunch of keys that were lying next to the TV on the cabinet. "Now I understand." She then proceeded to unlock all three of the locks and opened the tall gate.

Without hesitation, Koko came out of the room and over to where I sat. She gently took my arm, pulled me to my feet, and led me back through the gate and into her house. Plopping down with her back against the wall, she indicated she would like me to do the same.

Penny had briefed me on what to expect from Koko. "She's gentle. But I should tell you—right now she's very interested in boobs."

As I sat down opposite her, Koko reached out to finger the collar of my blouse. Not to pull it—she was just investigating. But then she unbuttoned my top button.

"No," I said. "We don't do that, Koko."

So Koko stopped but still held my collar. It was as if she was going to rebutton my blouse, but she didn't. So I did.

Then I rested my hands on her fat tummy, and I could feel the rough black hair. My zookeeper friends had often told me that when working around gorillas, one should avoid making direct eye contact, lest it be interpreted as a challenge. Well, in this case there was no avoiding it. Here we sat, this beautiful girl and I, gazing into each other's eyes and both obviously enjoying the moment completely. For Koko, this just seemed like natural conversation!

While all this was going on, Penny and her photographer, Ronald Cohn, were snapping pictures, for which I am eternally grateful, since I would never have been able to convince myself—let alone anyone else—that this had actually taken place.

When people see these pictures, the first question is invariably, "Weren't you petrified?!" In all honesty, I have to tell you I was so completely caught up in this unbelievable experience that fear never entered my mind.

Can you imagine the absolute trust Penny has to have in this animal? Koko was dealing with a total stranger—not her familiar and beloved Dr. Patterson.

And she was taking that stranger into her own private territory while a relaxed Penny sat outside, taking pictures and writing down Koko's reactions.

Koko and I visited for about twenty minutes. At one point, she got up and disappeared into the back of the house. After a moment, she returned, carrying a toy alligator that was about a foot long. As she handed the toy to me, she frowned and shivered her shoulders. I really didn't need Penny's explanation that I was being told that the alligator was "scary." Koko made it very clear.

I have been back to see this wonderful creature three times, and can't wait to go again. The last time I was there, Koko kept rubbing her fingers across her mouth—and now I did need Penny's translation.

"She recognizes you." Penny laughed. "And she has named you 'Lipstick.' Not many of her visitors actually wear lipstick."

We recently celebrated Koko's thirty-seventh birthday. Koko, dear: As smart as you are, you haven't learned as much from us as we are learning from you.

STUFFED
ANIMALS

*N*ow, here is a subject I should stay away from or I risk having a net thrown over me—but since we've come this far, I'll chance it.

You won't be surprised to learn that I love stuffed animals. Both at my home in Los Angeles and at my house in Carmel there is a special room devoted to them, filled to capacity. I especially love the exotic ones—there is an anteater, a rhinoceros, a beluga whale, an armadillo, a bear—not a Teddy, a <u>grizzly</u>—the list goes on.

Where it begins to get a little weird is that to me,

these stuffed animals are almost real. They have their individual personalities—some are looking right into my eyes—and when a new member joins the group, I introduce him to the others. The animals have been collected over the years—I don't actually go out and buy them.

My fax machine is also in that room, so I go in and out often. (I keep the door closed, because Ponti [aka Pontiac, my golden retriever] thinks anything stuffed with cotton is his territory.) Well, I never enter that room without speaking to the animals. "Hi, guys!" And I never leave it without saying, "See you later. I love you." <u>Out loud!</u> *[Editor's Note: I am eighty-nine years old!]*

Ponti isn't the only reason the door remains closed. That also happens to be the catchall room that keeps me awake at night.

It shouldn't surprise you that I don't often tell anyone what I have just revealed.

Let's keep it between us.

With a real live tiger cub!

NBCU Photo Bank

BEETHOVEN

Have you ever petted a hard-boiled egg? An enormous one that's in your lap? I have, and it was one of the happiest experiences of my life.

Not long ago, I spent some time in Atlanta, Georgia, filming a movie, *The Lost Valentine*, with Jennifer Love Hewitt and Sean Faris. As a rule, I try to avoid going on location—being away from home and Ponti is not my favorite thing. However, this was such a good script, and the cast—Jennifer and Sean—was almost irresistible. There was something else that influenced my decision, which you might find strange—Atlanta is home to a famous aquarium.

I have worked with the Monterey Bay Aquarium in California since its inception. It is one of the state-of-the-art organizations known worldwide, as is the Georgia Aquarium in Atlanta. I had heard so much about that facility and was thrilled to have a chance to see it. On my first day off of filming, a tour was arranged.

Well, like Monterey, the Atlanta Aquarium has earned and lives up to its reputation. It is a beautiful aquarium, a great learning center, and one of the most popular attractions in that lovely city. It was gratifying to see the support it received from the crowds of visitors absorbing the message of how fragile our abused oceans have become and what we, as individuals, can do to help the situation.

The first amazing thing you see as you enter is a huge whale shark swimming in an enormous pool. A bridge enables you to stand and watch this incredible creature as he crosses beneath you. He must be about twenty feet long and heavy-set—the biggest animal I have ever seen. That would have made the whole trip for me, but the best was yet to come.

I visited the seals and sea lions, who were enthusiastic hosts. And then I was taken to another pool even larger than the first. There, I was introduced to a very nice trainer, and I could see there was action on the other side of the pool but we were too far away to see what it was. The trainer, whose name is Dennis Christian, asked if I would like to meet their beluga whales.

How is that for the silliest question ever?

Following instructions, I rolled up the cuffs of my slacks, stepped into a pair of waders, and donned a plastic overcoat. This must have been a private area, as there was no one else around as Dennis led me along the edge of the pool. Walking in the waders was awkward, and the ledge was narrow.

I didn't mention that I can't swim.

We hadn't gone far when Dennis stopped and asked me to sit down on the deck at the edge of the pool. Once I was settled and secure, he called out, "Beethoven! Come meet Betty!"

He said it only once, but immediately something big came swimming across the pool—right up to my knees. Wearing a big smile, this giant white head came out of the water and almost onto my lap.

Dennis said, "It's okay to touch him if you want to."

Want to? I reached out and stroked the huge head, which felt like a hard rubber ball but looked for all the world like the aforementioned hard-boiled egg. His head was so big I had to look into his eyes, which were very small and bright, one at a time, and he looked right back into mine.

The trainer made the introductions, then said, in a most ordinary conversational tone, "Beethoven, want to show Betty your teeth?"

The white face opened to reveal a large cavern containing a row of white teeth—not jagged or pointy but almost similar to dentures. I was directed to run my finger around them, and I was amazed that this gorgeous creature took it in stride. Remembering my exchanges with elephants, I gently slapped the big pink tongue, and, sure enough, Beethoven made it clear that he thoroughly enjoyed it.

After a few minutes of this wonderful visit, Dennis said, "All right, Beethoven, you go back and send Mauris over."

Again, he directed the animal only once, still without raising his voice, and in immediate response Beethoven backed away, turned around, and swam to the other side of the pool, where Kim, the girl trainer, sat. As he reached her, another beautiful beluga headed our way. This was the female, Mauris. Again, she greeted me but was a little more tentative. In a very few moments she relaxed, and we became friends.

Of course, I was on cloud nine.

During this whole once-in-a-lifetime experience, I was deeply impressed by the obvious rapport among these animals and their humans. It was clear to me that intellectual connection and trust were what enabled the whales' immediate response to instruction; this was more than a case of animals obeying orders.

They were obviously involved in the interchange. Nonthreatening communication laced with a measure of passion can accomplish wonders.

It can also result in a visitor falling in love with a great white whale.

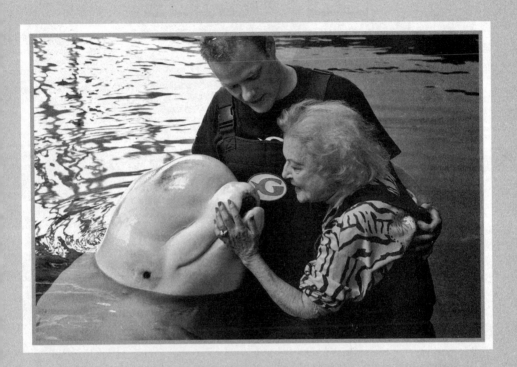

Photograph by Addison Hill

PET ADOPTION

I work with the Los Angeles Society for the Prevention of Cruelty to Animals often and if I'm having a meeting there, I always go through the shelter unannounced so they're not fixing it up for my benefit. I just want to see how it is day to day.

One day about eighteen years ago, I did just that en route to my meeting. After walking through and seeing all the animals, I was just about to exit when I noticed a cage on top of a cabinet with this beautiful little shih tzu in there.

I said, "Where did she come from?"

The director said, "She's not up for adoption yet. She's a cruelty case. A woman paid a lot of money for her at a pet store, but when she brought the dog home, the little girl was so sick she couldn't stand up. The woman took the dog back to the pet store, and they said, 'Oh, I'm so sorry, we'll take care of her and give you another dog.'"

Thank God, the woman went back the next day to see how the puppy was, and it was not being treated or nursed back to health—it was in the window for sale! In a badly managed pet shop, viruses run rampant from one animal to another, and the care (or lack thereof) compounds that.

The woman took the store to court, and that little shih tzu puppy closed the pet shop—all by herself!

The puppy, however, couldn't be adopted until the trial was settled, which took another three months. So during that time, the woman got another dog, because she wanted to adopt.

Meanwhile, at LASPCA I asked if they would let me know the minute the trial was settled and she was up for adoption.

Three months down the road, I got a call. They

said the time was up and the little dog was eligible for adoption.

I said, "When can I pick Panda up?"

I hadn't even been thinking of a name—it just came out. Panda. At the time I had two male dogs—a little bichon frise rescue and a mini black poodle. I worried that Panda would come in and be intimidated, but the introduction went smoothly—to the point that I could almost hear her say, "All right, boys. There are going to be a few changes in town. I'm now in charge!" And she took over and ran the house until she was sixteen and three-fourths.

With my poodle Timothy.

SPEAKING
ANIMAL

I grew up with pets. In our house, they were more than pets—they were members of the family.

During the Depression, my dad made radios to sell to make extra money. Nobody had any money to buy the radios, so he would trade them for dogs. He built kennels in the backyard, and he cared for the dogs.

Now, radios didn't eat, but the dogs did. So it was not the best business venture.

At one point we got up to something like fifteen dogs—well-loved dogs. We'd rotate them through the house in shifts, but it was clear it was not really a good plan, and we found homes for everybody but one chow and one Pekingese whom we couldn't part with.

As far back as I can remember, my parents had animals.

My mother always told the story about Toby, their orange-marmalade cat that they had when I was born. Toby would sit on the edge of my crib, and Mom said that if Toby hadn't approved of the new baby when I came home from the hospital, I would have been sent right back.

When my folks first came to California, we lived in Pasadena for a while. And we had a white Angora kitty named Patsy. I remember her very clearly. I don't remember the kids across the street I used to play with, but I remember Patsy. I must have been five years old.

One day I went into the closet and came out screaming for my mother, "Patsy broke!! Patsy broke!!"

She'd had a litter of kittens, and I thought she'd come apart.

Interestingly, neither of my parents had pets growing up. But together they fell in love with animals—and, of course, it caught.

Two years ago I lost Panda at sixteen and three-fourths, and my ten-year-old golden, Kitta, and my eleven-year-old Himalayan kitty, Bob Cat. (If you didn't like cats you called him Mr. Cat.)

I lost them all within two months, and I was just devastated.

I work closely with the organization Guide Dogs for the Blind and sponsor a guide dog every Christmas. When they heard I lost Kitta, they called me and said they had a golden career-change dog if I would be interested.

I explained, "I really am so distraught at this point, I need closure. I just absolutely can't imagine adopting a dog right now"—pause—"but maybe I'll come up and meet him."

The next morning, I got on a plane and flew to San Rafael and met him. And then I got back on the plane to go home and "think it over."

Did you ever hear anything more ridiculous? You meet a golden retriever and you're going to go home and "think it over"? Who was I kidding? I couldn't get my phone out of my purse fast enough when we landed.

And that's my Pontiac. He was already named. Guide dog puppies in a litter all have the same first initial. Since he was a *P* litter (no pun intended), they named him Pontiac. I like to think of it as the Indian chief, not the car. Matter of fact, when the car company folded, I sat him down and carefully explained it was not his fault. For which I got a kiss.

Ponti went into career change because he had a bum leg. Some people say these dogs "flunked out" of school, but I absolutely refuse to use that expression. These dogs never "flunked" at <u>anything</u>.

Ponti is my only pet right now.

I want a kitty, and I want a little dog <u>so</u> bad. But I must be home to integrate them. I never took classes to learn how to integrate animals. I think I just learned it organically.

I speak better animal language than human language. I can read them like a book—although not as well as they can read me.

But with my schedule the way it is, I'm just waiting for time to supervise the introductions. That's on my bucket list.

Now, I also have an age problem. I'm eighty-nine years old. I've outgrown my last puppy, but I don't want Ponti to be my last dog. My friends Tom and Patty Sullivan have arranged that whatever pets I leave, they will take. They won't find homes for them, they will take them in and love them.

I can't imagine being without animals. And there are

so many older dogs that need homes desperately. So that's where I'll look, and we can grow older together.

And then there are cats. Cats are not remote. People who think cats are that way may never have lived with a cat. My Bob, for instance. If my knee was bent, he was on my lap or on my shoulder in a flash. He followed me around the house like a dog. In bed at night, I'd reach over to turn the light out and he'd be there. For eleven years I fell asleep with that purr on my shoulder. Cats love you very much—they are just more subtle about it.

You're never too old to adopt a pet if you look ahead and make arrangements for their future. Then relax and enjoy each other.

With another "planted" pet.

STATE OF
AFFAIRS

NAMES

*H*aving spent so many years memorizing lines, I am pretty good at remembering names. ("Pretty good" is probably a euphemism.)

My problem is <u>faces</u>. They just don't seem to register. I have no memory for faces at all. Consequently, at those gatherings where you are introduced to several people at the same time, I wind up with a bunch of names I can remember but I don't know where to put them. I try to make silent notes in my head: JohnSmithbluetie. JaneJonespearlearrings. Sometimes those notes can carry you through a whole evening before they evaporate.

That game may work with total strangers but not with someone you've met before and should remember but don't. You are off to a bad start when you say, "It's nice meeting you." And they respond with, "Yes, it's nice seeing you <u>again</u>."

An added hazard in my line of work is when the name you can't come up with happens to be that of a celebrity. Everyone else in the room knows that name—except you! As the celebrity approaches, it's too late to ask someone nearby for help. You can't ask the celeb or you'll hurt his ego. Just pray you don't have to make any introductions.

There are too many examples in real life to mention—that awkward moment when I just don't know someone's name happens all the time!

People approach you out of context—people you've not seen in years. Or they approach in groups. Or they've aged or changed their hair color or put on weight—making recognition even more difficult. I still will introduce myself in these situations—"Hi, I'm Betty White"—in the hopes they'll do the same. Invariably, they not only don't reciprocate, they look at me as if I'm out of my mind.

The 2011 SAG Awards was a classic example. There I was, in a room filled with actors from popular movies and shows all across television. They're celebrities. And I don't know who they are! You feel like you're on the edge of a cliff the entire night.

And in this industry, our business makes for an instant familiarity. All night, people approached me and said, "Oh, hello, Betty—I loved you in *Saturday Night Live*" or "*Hot in Cleveland* is great," and so on. And I don't know the person from Adam—though I most probably should.

You can't cover all the bases, but you wish you could cover a few.

The worst part is, a lot of people don't take kindly to your not remembering. But you're fighting as hard as you can. You've used up all of the clichéd ways of avoiding the situation, but you still can't grasp the name in question.

One time I tried what I thought was a great way to learn that elusive moniker. I asked, "How do you spell your last name?"

The answer came back, "With an i."

Great.

Whatever memory trick you employ, it is well worth the effort. People are often surprised and pleased when you call them by name—especially in a crowd.

One more complication is added for me as my hearing dims: I may not hear the name clearly in the initial introduction, and the only thing worse than forgetting a name is calling someone by the wrong one.

You are probably thinking that if I let a big party be all that work, why don't I just stay home? <u>Great idea!</u> And I usually do.

The operative word here is "big." I thoroughly enjoy a small group of friends—six, or maybe even eight. You can get into stimulating conversation, laugh together, disagree on occasion, and, if you're not careful, even learn something.

And you don't have to bother with all those name games.

See—I'm not quite as antisocial as I sound. Not quite.

With George Burns—a face and a name
you could never forget.

DINING ROOM TABLE

My desk, and what was originally intended to be my office, is located in a spare bedroom upstairs. The fax machine lives there, as well as my stuffed animals and piles and piles of books people send me in the hopes I'll take a look at them for endorsement or out of curiosity or for pleasure. I'm too busy to read much of anything lately, but it's against my religion to throw out a book, so they keep stacking up and stacking up. It's gotten to the point that whenever Donna needs to fax something, I find myself saying, "No, no, let me do that!" so she doesn't have to see the messy room.

As that room filled up, I found that I kept bringing my work downstairs to the dining room table at the end of the living room. It sits by a big window looking out to the garden, and Donna and I find it a most pleasant workplace. Unfortunately, the table keeps getting piled higher and higher with leftover works in progress that have become virtually permanent. The dining room table has become an echo of the upstairs spare bedroom!

At four a.m., which seems to be my witching hour, I wake up not in a panic about memorizing my lines or what the day on the set might bring. No, I wake up haunted by that mess in that office—and the growing mess on my dining room table!

I think to myself, *Betty, you <u>must</u> clean this mess before you die.* God forbid someone else has to rifle through what's piled on there. I fantasize about bringing in giant garbage bags and just tossing everything out—but I can't bring myself to do it.

What about my potential dinner guests? With no place to serve them, we wind up with cocktails and hors d'oeuvres in the den, then we go out to eat. I am not what might be called one of the world's greatest hostesses.

One of my New Year's resolutions will be to finally clear that table.

But not this year.

Ironically, I could hear very well back then.

ENTOURAGE

So many stars have staff, and I'm often asked about mine.

I have a wonderful housekeeper, Edna, who's been with me for almost twenty-five years. She's been with me so long I couldn't possibly ask her to retire. But she's slowing down like we all are. So a few years ago I hired her a cleaning lady named Anita.

If I have to do anything on the weekend, like attend a poker game, which means driving down to Newport

Beach, Anita will come in and feed Ponti and help me out. It's a very comfortable situation.

When it's not comfortable is when something happens like what happened the other morning. I woke up early, as usual, to go to the *Hot in Cleveland* table read. I made Ponti his dish of food and stepped outside to put it down for him. Just then the wind picked up and slammed the door shut behind me, locking me out. I have an elaborate system of keys hidden to get me back into the house, but when I went to find the final key, it was missing. Luckily, I'd gotten far enough inside that there was a phone in the room. So I had to call Glenn Kaplan, my business manager, who lives nearby. Glenn has an extra set of my house keys, and fortunately he was still home. But his copies of my keys were in his office so he had to drive there to get them and bring them back up to me.

By the time he got to me, I'd been almost exclusively outside for forty-five minutes in nothing but my bathrobe. And you can imagine how glamorous I looked when he arrived!

My dear friend Jerry Martin used to have a set of keys to my house, too, and he used to take care to visit Ponti when I was on set. In fact, I'd never have been able to film *The Proposal* without Jerry's assistance.

When I was first called about the role, I was told the filming was supposed to take ten weeks in Boston. I said I couldn't possibly leave for that long. But then the schedule was cut down to six weeks, and Jerry volunteered to visit Ponti every day. I managed to make it back a couple of times on weekends, so between the two of us, along with Edna and Anita, I felt that Ponti was covered as he adores them all.

Sadly, we lost Jerry very suddenly a few weeks ago.

I not only miss him deeply but on a morning like the one when I locked myself out, I start wondering about the wisdom of my staffing situation! Should I have more help? But I so enjoy being alone.

That said, the other downside to my system is that I slip behind a little all the time. I <u>never</u> finish a day and think, *I'm all caught up.*

Then what am I doing writing a book? I needed to write a book at this time in my life like I needed another hole in my head.

But I couldn't turn it down, it was such a temptation.

I told you up front that writing is my favorite thing.

POKER

I'm not a great poker player but I love to play.

Bob Stewart of Goodson/Todman, who created game shows like *Password*, *$25,000 Pyramid*, and more, hosts a poker game that he's run for more than fifty years. Bob and I have been friends for almost that long, and about fifteen years ago he invited me to deal in. Our group plays at the Newport Beach house of Ann Cullen, whose late husband, Bill Cullen, was also a great game-show host. We all giggle and scratch and have a wonderful time.

We don't play for big money, but we play for <u>blood</u>.

It's dealer's choice, and each hand is high/low. We don't play a lot of wild games. Screw Thy Neighbor (it's really Screw Your Neighbor, but we call it Screw <u>Thy</u> Neighbor, to class it up) is my favorite. You get a chance to keep a card or pass it along.

I think the only reason they let me into the game is that I usually leave about $13 on the table. We have a brass cup engraved with "Pico Poker Club," and whoever comes out ahead at the end of the night takes this cup home. The winner can enjoy the cup until the next game, but God forbid you don't return it then. The penalty for that offense is $2,000 or death, whichever is most appropriate.

One day, Henry Polic, who lives in the Valley, was almost to Ann's and realized he'd forgotten the cup. He turned around and must have done some creative driving to get home to pick it up and make it back in time for the game.

Just as we were wondering where Henry was, he raced in, breathless. "I can't afford the penalty!" he said, and we all burst out laughing.

I love to play cards and rarely have anybody to play with anymore.

So these games are precious.

On Match Game—*I've always loved a great game.*

MODERN
TECHNOLOGY

(Thoroughly Modern Betty?)

*E*very time you begin to think you're such a contemporary and you don't feel your age, you realize you don't own a computer!—and intend to keep it that way.

There are a few reasons for this.

I get a lot of mail, as I've mentioned before. Donna does most of the fan mail, but the volume of my personal mail, too, is enormous! I come in with an armful every day and sort it into different stacks. I may push one stack aside, but before I do, I at least have an idea of what's <u>in</u> that stack. If I had a computer and clicked a button to "store" something, I wouldn't sleep at night! I'd wonder what was stored in there, did I answer this or that or the other? That scares me. I think of it as the computer equivalent of my upstairs office and dining room table.

And many people use computers to write. They talk about how efficient it is, how fast. But I can't create with a machine. As I said in "Writer's Block," there's a connection from my brain to the paper through my longhand writing that just works for me.

When my agent and publisher and I got together to work on this book, my publisher worked with an amazing instrument I had never seen—a computerized pen that recorded audio and plugged into the computer. A <u>talking</u> pen? I named it Bruce.

It's a far cry from that first book I ever wrote when I was a kid, which was one hundred pages in longhand, written with a pen you dipped in ink!

Thank you, Bruce. I don't deserve you.

CHILDREN

When I was a little girl, my mother loved baby dolls. She collected them.

But my toys were always animals.

I would spend all my lunch money on little blown-glass animal families at the toy store, which I later had to spend a lot of time dusting.

Barbara Walters once asked me if I ever had desired to have a child.

The answer is, I never did think about it.

I know there are many career girls today who would

disagree, but I'm not a big believer in being able to do both. I think somebody takes the short end of the stick.

I had such a wonderful rapport with my folks, but my mother didn't work. She was home with me.

It's an individual choice. I didn't think I could do justice to both career and motherhood, maybe because I had the mother I did. It's <u>such</u> an individual choice.

And I'm a stepmother. I have the best stepchildren in the world.

When Allen and I first married, I became the stepmother of teenagers. Never having had children, I was suddenly the mother of teens! But we got along great. So great, they called me "Dragon Lady," lovingly.

Even after all these years, we love each other dearly, and I am most proud of the children this career girl inherited. A major blessing—yet again.

SINCE YOU ASKED . . .

Holding the 2011 Screen Actors Guild
Award for Outstanding Performance by a
Female Actor in a Comedy Series.

KEVIN MAZUR/WIREIMAGE

INTEGRITY

*I*t's important to maintain as level a head as possible in this exciting business over the years.

The toughest time is when you're on a roll . . . when everything is going phenomenally well, like it is for me right now.

That's when you have to remember that image in the mirror and not let success get to you. It is important that you not believe your own publicity. Be grateful for whatever praise you receive, but take it with a grain of salt.

You have to keep your feet on the ground and remember that this is what you've worked for all your life. And now that you've achieved it, you don't want to screw it up. You can't get carried away with your image, because you know better than anyone else who the <u>real</u> person is.

You don't just luck into integrity. You work at it.

ADVICE
COLUMN

One of the first interview questions always is:
What advice would you give young actresses
coming into this business?

The answer is:

Treat your profession with respect.

Come in prepared.

Walk in to every situation with a positive, open
mind. Allow yourself time to experience a situation before forming an opinion.

To abuse our profession by partying or getting into

trouble or copping an attitude like some people do is the height of ingratitude, in my opinion.

To not be grateful for what you've been blessed with, knowing how many people in the world would sell their souls to do what you do, or to abuse it is, I think, unconscionable.

In the acting profession and the sporting world, young people are exposed to more temptation, more everything, because they have a whole bunch more money than do young people in other jobs. They're getting these phenomenal salaries; sometimes it's too easy to slip into bad behavior. Bad stuff.

I hate to sound like I'm pontificating, but it's hard to write a book without sounding that way from time to time. When you're blessed to do the thing you love to do and you're making a lot of money at it so you can benefit your passion, that's a pretty great formula. Appreciate it—don't abuse it.

If you're not enthusiastic, just lie down and close your eyes and be <u>very</u> quiet.

With Jennifer Love Hewitt.

ERIC HEINILA/CBS/NEWSCOM

On The Late Late Show *with Craig Ferguson.*

I'M EIGHTY-NINE?

One thing they don't tell you about growing old—you don't feel old, you just feel like yourself. And it's true. I don't _feel_ eighty-nine years old. I simply _am_ eighty-nine years old.

If I didn't feel so well, I might have a different philosophy altogether.

But I fall into traps sometimes.

Let's say I meet someone I find attractive. I have to keep reminding myself of how old I am, because I don't _feel_ like I'm that old. I fight the urge to flirt and try to shape up. No fool like an old fool.

But I don't get depressed as the number climbs. Perhaps because I don't fear death. To some it is such a bête noire that it ruins some of the good time they have left.

Estelle Getty was so afraid of dying that the writers on *The Golden Girls* couldn't put a dead joke in the script. This was early on—long before she ever got ill.

Again, I'm quoting my mother, but her take on the subject I thought was great. She said we know so much and can discover so much more, but what <u>no one</u> knows for sure is what exactly happens when we pass on. When we'd lose someone we would grieve, of course, but she would say, "Now he knows the secret." Somehow that helped the pain for me.

And now—<u>she</u> knows the secret.

If you've ever lost a loved one, or witnessed it, you can't help but see that the body is an envelope for the letter.

My friends kid me that when it happens to me, Allen's going to be up there waiting for me and probably my mom and dad. That's my family. But before I can get to them I'm going to have to wade through Booty and Binky and Bob and Panda and Kitta and all my pets through the years—

Picturing that always starts me laughing.

Donald Sanders/Globe Photos

Afterword

If you have stuck with me this far I say a big thank you. Hope you enjoyed the trip. If not, take comfort in the fact that I had a wonderful time.

Love,

Betty